FIFTY WAYS TO TEACH YOUNG LEARNERS

TIPS FOR ESL/EFL TEACHERS

LESLEY ITO

50 Ways to Teach Young Learners: Tips for ESL/EFL Teachers

Copyright © 2013 by Lesley Ito; revised 2018

All rights reserved. No part of this publication may be reproduced, stored in or introduced into a retrieval system, or transmitted, in any form, or by any means (electronic, mechanical, photocopying, recording, or otherwise) without the prior written permission of the copyright owner. Dramatic works contained within this volume are intended only as reading material, and their inclusion does not imply the granting of performance licenses, which must be arranged through the author.

Edited by Dorothy E. Zemach. Cover design by DJ Rogers. Photos by Lesley Ito.

Published in the United States by Wayzgoose Press.

CONTENTS

How To Use This Book   vii
Introduction   ix

Part I
VOCABULARY ACTIVITIES

1. Colored Paper Flutter   3
2. Finger Shapes   5
3. I See Something Yellow   9
4. Number Writing Chain   11
5. Simple Math   13
6. Months of the Year Dice Game   15
7. Rooms Guessing Game   17
8. People Who Live In My House   19
9. Emotions Guessing Game   21
10. Classroom Objects Telescope Activity   23
11. Rocket Blast Off   25
12. Food Class Survey   27
13. Vegetables and Fruit Color Sorting   29
14. Please   30
15. Places in My City   32
16. Weather Dice Game   34
17. Vehicle Counting Game   36
18. Occupations Guessing Game   38

Part II
SONGS, CHANTS, AND TPR ACTIVITIES

19. First Day of Class Song   43
20. In, On, Under TPR Chant   45
21. Color Chant   48

22. New Version of Head, Shoulders, Knees, and Toes — 50
23. TPR Days of the Week — 52
24. TPR Time — 56
25. Adjective Chant — 58
26. Morning Routine TPR Song — 60

Part III
FLASHCARD GAMES

27. Flashcards in a Bag — 63
28. Flashcard Marching Game — 64
29. Memory — 65
30. Fetch the Card — 67
31. Cross the Dangerous Bridge! — 68

Part IV
GRAMMAR ACTIVITIES

32. Is it a ____? / Is it an ____? Guessing Game — 71
33. Singular/Plural Noun Practice — 73
34. What is it? / What are they? Around the Table Activity — 74
35. This/That, These/Those Drawing Activity — 76
36. His/Her Drawing Activity — 78
37. Can you ____? Animal Game — 79

Part V
COMBINATION ACTIVITIES

38. It's/They're, Clothing, and Other Things We Wear — 83
39. House Dice Game — 85
40. My Birthday and Holidays — 87
41. Prepositions Dice Game — 88
42. Animal Body Parts — 90
43. Animal Guessing Game — 91
44. Store — 92

45. Treasure Hunt	94

Part VI
HOLIDAY ACTIVITIES

46. Christmas Presents	97
47. Christmas Phonics	99
48. Jack-o'-Lantern Bag Craft/Trick or Treating	100
49. Halloween Phonics	102
50. My Holiday	103
Bonus tip!	105

HOW TO USE THIS BOOK

Most teachers use a textbook in class, which provides both instruction and practice – but, often, not enough practice. Students need to practice again and again, and in different ways, not just to keep their interest but to both learn and remember. Also keep in mind that young learners enjoy variety. It can be challenging for a busy teacher to find new ways to practice the same material.

This book gives you ideas to help teach young learners in English. It can be used with any textbook, or without any textbook at all.

Not every idea will work for every student or for every class. That's why there are fifty. We feel sure that many of the ideas presented here will bring you results if you try them sincerely and practice them regularly.

Here is a suggested method for using this book:

1. Read through all of the fifty tips without stopping.
2. Read through the tips again. Choose five or six that you think might work for your class. Decide when you will try them.
3. Choose different types of ideas: Some that focus on vocabulary; some that focus on grammar; some that use physical actions; some that use songs and chants.
4. Each time you use one of the ways, make a note about how well it worked for you and why. Remember that most of the tips will work best if you use them several times (or even make them a habit). Don't try a tip only once and decide and decide it's no good for your students. Give the tips you try at least a few chances.
5. Every few weeks, read through the tips again, and choose some new ones. Discontinue using any methods that are not working for you and your students.

If you also teach adults or older children, consider trying some of the other books in our *50 Ways to Teach* series, that focus on individual skills. However, no one skill in English is really separate from the others. Speaking, listening, reading, writing, vocabulary, and grammar are all connected. Students who improve in one area will almost always improve in other areas, too.

INTRODUCTION

This book is both for teachers who are new to ESL/EFL and teachers who are looking for effective activities for their young learner English classes. This isn't an exploration of research and pedagogy, but a list of easy-to-do, classroom-tested activities for children that require little preparation.

Not all these ways may work for your class exactly as written. However, it is always a good idea to look at an idea and think about how you could adapt it to fit your own context. When you read an idea, think about how you could change it to fit your students' ages, levels, culture, and interests. Please feel free to adapt the activities in any way you like.

When considering trying the activities in this book, think about your course goals and objectives, and which activities would be most useful in helping you reach them. Some of these activities can be modified to accompany or supplement a textbook; others provide opportunities to go beyond what your textbook might provide.

This book is divided into 6 categories:

1. Vocabulary Activities
2. Songs, Chants, and TPR Activities
3. Flashcard Games
4. Grammar Activities
5. Combination Activities
6. Holiday Activities

All the activities in this book are developmentally appropriate for children. Sometimes, teachers forget that children are not "mini-adults," and that they learn things in a different way. It is best to use activities that exploit their sense of wonder and imagination, that involve the body, and make the learning process fun. These activities require little preparation and use typical classroom or household items, such as dice, construction paper, or paper plates.

I

VOCABULARY ACTIVITIES

It's important for young learners to have a large vocabulary when learning a foreign language. Knowing many words is essential to building up listening skills and speaking skills. When young learners encounter chunks of language, they are learning both grammar and the new vocabulary words within the chunk. When children learn to read, having a large oral vocabulary in the target language will help them enormously. Vocabulary (especially nouns and verbs) is one of the easiest things to teach young learners, and they are eager to learn new words.

However, some teachers seem to think that the only way to teach vocabulary is to drill with flashcards. While this might be an efficient way to introduce vocabulary, the students (and perhaps the teacher!) will soon become bored and quickly forget what was learned.

To effectively teach vocabulary, engage the students' sense of fun and encourage them to use their imagination. It's also important to allow them to move their bodies and to move around props, such as flashcards or toys, when doing an activity. These activities can also be used as a fun way to pre-teach the vocabulary before a lesson.

COLORED PAPER FLUTTER

After pre-teaching colors:

- Cut up different colors of construction paper into small squares. Put them in an opaque file or bag.
- Open the file or bag, look inside, and gasp as if you are surprised. Do this two more times to get the children interested in what's inside.
- Ask a child if they want to see what is inside. When they say yes, pretend you are going to show them; but instead, pour the cards on the floor or table, saying, "Oh no!"
- Motion for the children to come help you pick them up. Choose one card and say what color it is. Chant that color name over and over as the students pick up cards of that color.
- Once all the cards of that color are picked up, choose a new color and repeat the activity.

4 | FIFTY WAYS TO TEACH YOUNG LEARNERS

Continue the process with each color until all the cards have been picked up.
- Thank the students for helping you clean up the cards!

Note: Repeat this activity! Children love to do this many times, even if they know what is going to happen, and will most likely laugh more the second time.

FINGER SHAPES

Children love making shapes with their fingers. You can say the word, and have children make the shapes, to test listening comprehension. Have them repeat the word after you a few times for pronunciation. Call on children to say a shape for the rest of the class to make. Here are some examples on the following pages.

6 | FIFTY WAYS TO TEACH YOUNG LEARNERS

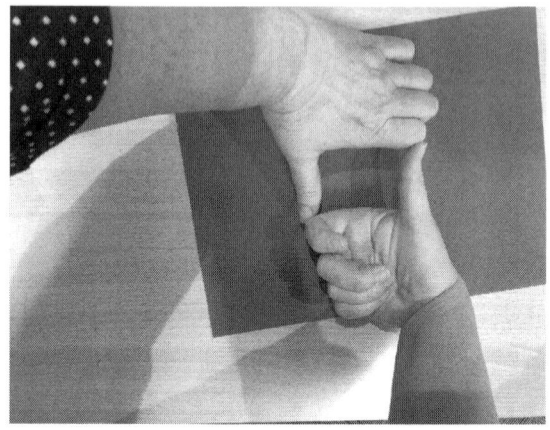

Square

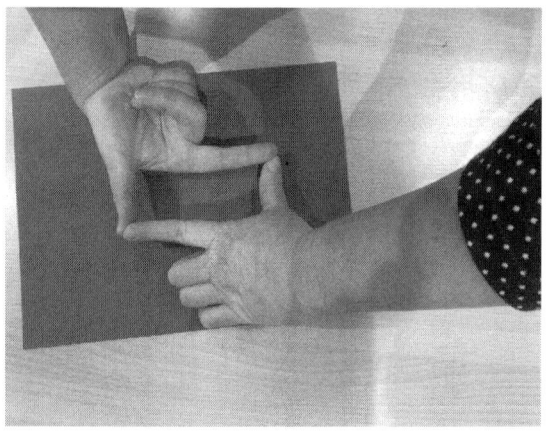

Rectangle

FINGER SHAPES | 7

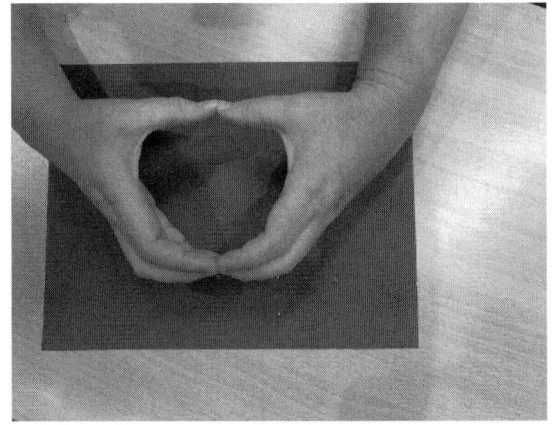

Circle

Heart

8 | FIFTY WAYS TO TEACH YOUNG LEARNERS

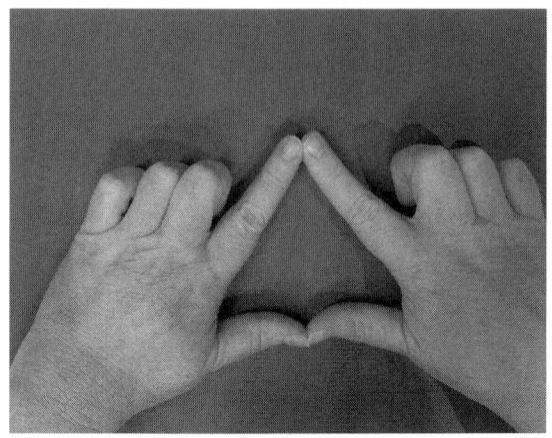

Triangle

Star: This takes teamwork – three students to work together

3

I SEE SOMETHING YELLOW

To practice colors, have students stand up. Say, *I see something (color)*. Students have to find something in the classroom with that color and point to it. Do this once for each color you've taught. Once students get used to the game, they can take over the teacher's role by choosing a color and saying, *I see something (color)*.

Variation: Have students guess the one object you are thinking of. They can ask, *Is it this?* and point. You respond with *Yes, it is* or *No, it isn't*. They can also use the name of the object if they know it. *Is it the eraser? Is it the whiteboard?*

4

NUMBER WRITING CHAIN

Pre-teach numbers. Have students line up in front of the board. Give the first student in line a piece of chalk or a whiteboard marker. Say a number. The student listens and writes that number on the board, gives the chalk or marker to the next student in line, and goes to the end of the line. Repeat until all students have had a chance to write a number on the board.

Then, write a few extra numbers on the board. Give the first student in line an eraser. Ask the second student in line to call out one of the numbers on the board. The first student in line listens and erases the correct number, then hands the eraser to the next student, and goes to the end of the line. Repeat until all students have had a chance to erase a number.

What can you do about the numbers that are left over on the board? Point to them, ask the students to call them out, and if they are correct, erase them.

5

SIMPLE MATH

Get six sheets of white paper. Fold a piece of paper into eight equal sections and cut them out to make cards. You'll need 47 cards in all.

Make four groups of number flashcards: Two sets of cards of the numbers 1 – 10, one set of cards with the numbers 2 – 20, four sets of cards with the + sign, and four sets of cards with the = sign. To save time, ask students to help you make the flashcards.

Ask students to use the cards to make their own math problems. For example, a student can put the following flashcards in order: 8 + 4 = 12. When she has created her own math problem, she says it aloud: *Eight plus four is twelve*. Once she is finished, she puts her cards back and lets another student try.

6

MONTHS OF THE YEAR DICE GAME

Pre-teach numbers 1 – 12 and the months of the year. Give students a pair of dice. Write the months of the year in order with a number next to them. For example, 1 – January, 2 – February, etc.

Students roll the dice and then call out the name of the month that corresponds to the number they rolled. Students can choose to roll one die or two (because obviously you can't roll a pair of dice and get a 1!).

After they call out the name of the month, erase it from the board. Students who roll a number for a month that has already been erased must call out the name of the month anyway, and then their turn is over.

The game ends when all the months of the year have been erased from the board.

ROOMS GUESSING GAME

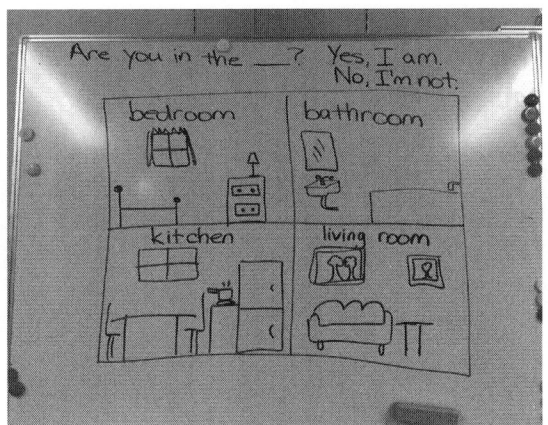

Draw a simple layout of a house on the board, or display a textbook or picture dictionary with a layout of rooms of a house. Pre-teach the rooms of a house. Write the following question and answers on the board and pre-teach them: *Are you in the _____? Yes, I am. / No, I'm not.*

One student comes to the front of the classroom and either whispers the name of a room in your ear or secretly points to it in the textbook or picture dictionary. Then, other students take turns guessing where this student is in the house, using the question you modeled on the board.

Once a student guesses correctly, and the student in the front answers, *Yes, I am*, the student who guessed right comes to the front, chooses a new room, and the game continues.

You can also play this game using the rooms in a school, places in a neighborhood, shops in a mall, cities in a country, etc.

8

PEOPLE WHO LIVE IN MY HOUSE

Pre-teach family member vocabulary using flashcards. Draw an outline of a house on a piece of scrap paper. Ask students, *Who lives in your house?*

Students take turns thinking about their own families and

then placing the appropriate flashcards in the outline of the house to show who lives in their house. Then they say the family member vocabulary on those cards.

Advanced students can say something like *My mother, father, sister, and grandmother live in my house with me.*

EMOTIONS GUESSING GAME

Get six small paper plates. Draw a simple facial expression on each. (I always draw a happy face, a sad face, a sleepy face, a surprised face, an angry face, and scared face – see example photos.) Teach the vocabulary as you draw the same faces on the board.

Write the following question and answers on the board and practice them: *Are you _____? Yes, I am. / No, I'm not.*

One student comes to the front of the classroom, secretly chooses one of the paper plates, and turns his back to the class. Once his back is turned, he places the plate over his face, like a mask. Then the other students take turns guessing which emotion he chose, using the question you modeled on the board.

Once a student guesses correctly and the student turns around, still holding the "mask" over his face to reveal the plate over his face and answers, *Yes, I am*, the student who guessed right comes to the front, chooses a new paper circle, and the game continues.

An angry face

10

CLASSROOM OBJECTS TELESCOPE ACTIVITY

Gather real classroom objects that you want students to learn. Teach the vocabulary as you place them randomly around the room. Roll up a piece of scrap paper and put a piece of tape on it to make a "telescope."

Hold the telescope and pretend you are looking for one of the classroom objects. When you see one, gasp with feigned surprise and say what it is (*Look! It's a dictionary!*).

Then pass the telescope to another student and let them search for a new classroom object. Continue until all the students have had a chance to use the telescope.

ROCKET BLAST OFF

Students can usually count to ten without thinking, but can they count backwards? When you count backwards, you have to think about the numbers.

Ask students to stand up and then squat, while holding their hands over their head, fingertips touching to make the shape of a rocket.

Then, count down from 10 to 1 together. End like this: … *three, two, one… blast off!* Everyone stands up with arms stretched up and pretends to be a rocket blasting into the atmosphere.

FOOD CLASS SURVEY

Each student chooses a food and writes the following question about it on a piece of paper:

Do you like (food)?

Then, students stand up and ask all the other students in

their class if they like that food, keeping a record of how many people said they liked it and how many people didn't like it (by making tally marks on the paper).

After everyone has asked all their classmates, have each student take turns reporting how many students said "yes" and how many students said "no." Write the results on the board.

VEGETABLES AND FRUIT COLOR SORTING

Teach colors as you lay color flashcards or pieces of colored construction paper in different places on the table. Teach fruits and vegetables, either by using flashcards or plastic fruit and vegetable toys.

Then give each student a fruit or vegetable flashcard or toy and say, "Go!" Students have to look at the color of their fruit or vegetable and place it on the corresponding color card. Repeat until all the fruits or vegetables have been placed on color cards.

Then talk about which fruits and vegetables are what color. For example, *An apple, a tomato, and a strawberry are red. A banana is yellow.* Be sure to point out which colors don't have any fruit or vegetables on them. As a famous comedian once said, "There is no blue food!" (Except blueberries!)

14

PLEASE

This game is very similar to "Simon Says." However, most EFL learners do not know that "Simon" is a common man's name, and if they do, they wonder aloud why you must do what he says. (Yes, these are actual questions I've been asked by young learners.) I think it is more useful to teach them this polite and useful phrase: *(Action), please.*

Pre-teach basic verbal commands such as *Point to your nose* or *Jump!* Stand in front of the students. When you say an action and "please" (_____, *please*) and do the action, the student have to imitate you.

If you say an action and do the action without saying "please," the students are "out" and have to sit down.

Continue until only one student is standing. If time allows, let the student who won stand in front and take the place of the teacher.

PLACES IN MY CITY

Use flashcards to teach about places in a town. Show a flashcard and ask the students to say the name of the place in their area.

For example, if you show a "hospital" flashcard, ask them to say the name of a one nearby. Line up the flashcards and have the students place their erasers or some other small object in front of the first flashcard. (These lined up flashcards will be played like a board game.)

Students take turns rolling a die and moving their eraser across the line of flashcards, saying the name of the flashcard that they land on. If they can't say the name, have them move back one square at a time until they land on one they know (but remind them of the names of any they missed).

The student who makes it to the end of the line of flashcards is the winner, but keep playing until all students make it to the end.

WEATHER DICE GAME

Divide the whiteboard into six sections and number each section. Pre-teach the following weather vocabulary as you draw a simple picture of each into a section: *sunny*, *windy*, *rainy*, *snowy*, *cloudy*, *foggy*. Students take turns rolling a die and then saying the weather vocabulary word that corresponds to the number they rolled.

After they call out the weather, draw a big X in the square. Students who roll a number for weather that has been crossed out must call out the name of the weather anyway, and then their turn is over.

The game ends once all the weather words have been crossed out on the board.

WEATHER DICE GAME | 35

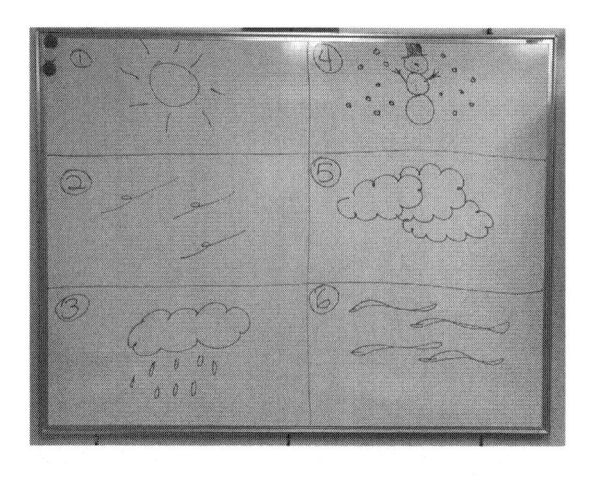

Weather pictures on the whiteboard

VEHICLE COUNTING GAME

Pre-teach vehicle vocabulary words (with flashcards, pictures, or toys) and then line the pictures or models up on the side of the table, where they can be easily touched by the students. Write *I go by* _____. on the board.

Have the students stand in line. Call out a number to the

first student in line. That student counts up to that number as she touches the vehicles in order. When she gets to the picture/toy that matches the number you called out, she says, *I go by (vehicle),* and go the end of the line.

Continue until all students have had a turn.

18

OCCUPATIONS GUESSING GAME

Pre-teach occupations using flashcards or a picture dictionary. Write the following question and answers on the board and pre-teach them: *Are you a _____? Yes, I am. / No, I'm not.*

One student comes up to the front of the classroom and secretly chooses a flashcard or points to an occupation in the picture dictionary. Then the other students take turns guessing what occupation the student is, using the question you modeled on the board.

Once a student guesses correctly, and the student in the front answers, *Yes, I am,* the student who guessed right comes to the front, chooses a new occupation, and the game continues.

II

SONGS, CHANTS, AND TPR ACTIVITIES

Children learn vocabulary and grammar in chunks of language, such as *My name is. . .* or *What time is it?* They can easily repeat these chunks if they are part of a classroom song or chant. Children may not be able to create original full sentences yet, but they can say a song or a chant. This is because children don't analyze the individual words in the language the way adult learners tend to do.

Another benefit of songs and chants are that they naturally teach children the correct rhythm and intonation of the language. As a teacher, don't worry if you are good at singing. It's not necessary to be a good singer to teach songs and chants; it's only necessary to be enthusiastic and enjoy yourself while singing or chanting. Chants are even more meaningful to students if they can play a role in creating a new version of a chant, using vocabulary they already know.

TPR is short for Total Physical Response. It is a language learning method where students move their body or touch something in response to something the teacher says. For example, if the teacher said, "Touch your head," students would touch their head with their hands. TPR activities are helpful for students who do not feel confident about speaking yet and prefer to express what they know in a non-verbal way. It also mimics the way very young children learn their first language.

FIRST DAY OF CLASS SONG

On the first day of class, try to spend a lot of time on activities that help students get to know each other better. Students will be less shy about speaking English in front of classmates they know well.

First, teach this simple song, sung to the tune of *Bingo* (start with the lines that go *B-I-N-G-O, B-I-N-G-O*, etc.):

> *1, 2, 3, 4, 5*
> *1, 2, 3, 4, 5*
> *1, 2, 3, 4, 5*
> *Hello, what's your name?*

Then, clasp your hands over your head, with your index fingers pointing towards the ceiling. Sing the song, and when you sing the *Hello, What's your name?* part, point to a student. That student says his name, and then points his fingers towards the ceiling, sings the song, and points to another student.

Continue until all students have said their name and have had a chance to sing. The last student can point to the teacher and ask the teacher's name again.

IN, ON, UNDER TPR CHANT

Teach the word *in* by making a loose fist with your left hand and sticking two fingers from your right hand into the middle of your fist. Teach *on* by making a tight fist with your left hand and laying the flat palm of your right hand on top of your fist. Teach *under* by making a tight fist with your left hand and laying the flat palm of your right hand under your fist. Now have everyone do the three motions one after the other while chanting, *In, on, under.*

46 | FIFTY WAYS TO TEACH YOUNG LEARNERS

position to demonstrate "in"

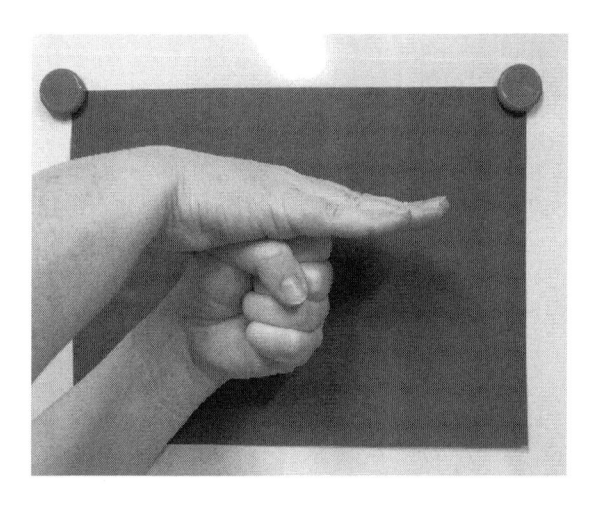

position to demonstrate "on"

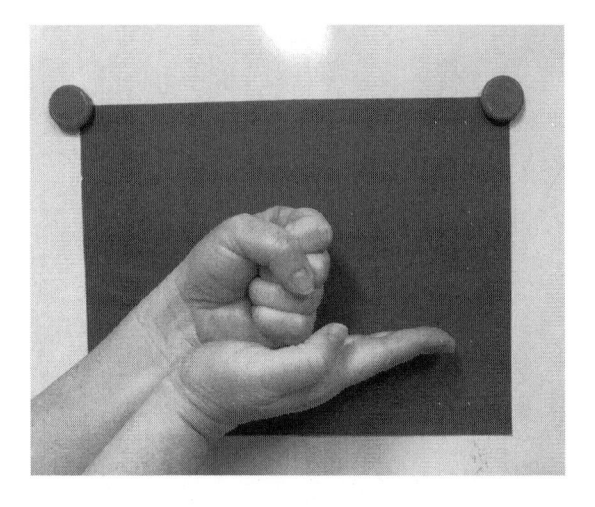

IN, ON, UNDER TPR CHANT | 47

position to demonstrate "under"

Once students have gotten used to making these motions, do the motions while singing the following song, to the tune of *Frère Jacques*:

> *In, on, under,*
> *In, on, under, ...*

(continue for the whole song)

COLOR CHANT

Choose a color. Write the following chant on the board:

> *(color), (color), (color).*
> *(blank space) is (color).*
> *(blank space) is (color), too.*
> *(blank space) is (color).*
> *(color), (color), (color).*

Elicit three things from students three things that are that color. If the students have trouble thinking of something, give them a picture dictionary to look at or have them look in their textbook.

Then write those words, draw a simple picture, or use a magnet to put a flashcard in the blank spaces in the chant. (If you decide to write the word, be sure to write an *a* or *an* in front of countable nouns.)

Here is an example for the color *green*:

Green, green, green.
A leaf is green.
A frog is green, too.
Lettuce is green.
Green, green, green.

NEW VERSION OF HEAD, SHOULDERS, KNEES, AND TOES

Head, Shoulders, Knees, and Toes is a classic song and TPR activity known to most teachers of children (but if you don't know it, check for it on YouTube and learn it!). As you sing the song, touch the different parts of your body mentioned in the song. Here's the original:

> *Head, shoulders, knees, and toes, knees and toes.*
> *Head, shoulders, knees, and toes, knees and toes.*
> *Eyes and ears and mouth and nose.*
> *Head, shoulders, knees, and toes, knees and toes.*

Students love this song, and also love to do it very quickly or very slowly. However, it does leave out quite a few body parts. Here is another version of the song:

> *Arms, stomach, legs, and feet, legs and feet.*
> *Arms, stomach, legs, and feet, legs and feet.*

Elbow, finger, neck, and back.
Arms, stomach, legs, and feet, legs and feet.

23

TPR DAYS OF THE WEEK

Using a calendar, teach the days of the week. Point out the first letter in each day of the week and write them down on the board: S M T W T F S. Then make the following poses to mimic the first letter of each day (one pose per page):

S for Sunday

TPR DAYS OF THE WEEK | 53

M for Monday

T for Tuesday

W for Wednesday

T for Thursday (a different T from Tuesday, for variety)

F for Friday

S for Saturday (a different S from Sunday, for variety)

Practice the days of the week as you make the poses. Then play a game where one student says the day of the week, and everyone has to make that pose.

24

TPR TIME

four o'clock

Pre-teach telling the time (only *o'clock* for lower-level students). Then students take turns holding up their arms like a clock face and asking, *What time is it?*

For example, if they put one arm straight up in the air and the other arm straight down and ask, *What time is it?*, the students would look at their arms and answer, *It's six o'clock.*

ADJECTIVE CHANT

Choose an adjective. Write the following chant on the board:

> *(adjective), (adjective), (adjective).*
> *(blank space) is (adjective).*
> *(blank space) is (adjective), too.*
> *(blank space) is (adjective).*
> *(adjective), (adjective), (adjective).*

Elicit from students three nouns that could be described by that adjective. If the students have trouble thinking of something, give them a picture dictionary to look at or have them look in their textbook.

Then write those words, draw a simple picture, or use a magnet to put a flashcard in the blank spaces in the chant. (If you decide to write the word, be sure to write *a* or *an* in front of countable nouns.)

Here is an example for the word *big*:

> *Big, big, big.*
> *A whale is big.*
> *A truck is big, too.*
> *An elephant is big.*
> *Big, big, big.*

MORNING ROUTINE TPR SONG

Pre-teach phrases pertaining to actions we do in the morning, such as

- *brush my teeth*
- *get dressed*
- *eat my breakfast*
- *comb my hair*
- *wash my face*
- *go to school*

Choose an action and sing the following song to the tune of *Here We Go 'Round the Mulberry Bush* (check YouTube if you don't know this song) as you act out that action:

> *This is the way I (action),*
> *(action), (action).*
> *This is the way I (action),*
> *So early in the morning.*

III

FLASHCARD GAMES

Flashcards are a great tool for teachers of young learners. The images on a flashcard can help teach children new vocabulary easily, and they are easy for teachers to store and carry. However, don't be under the misconception that flashcards can only be used for drilling vocabulary words. They can be used for all sorts of fun activities, from traditional games such as Memory to other games that involve the imagination.

Most textbooks or picture dictionaries offer flashcards you can buy or photocopy and make. You can also make your own flashcards using clip art or photos.

Flashcards will be subjected to a lot of wear and tear, so it is highly recommended that homemade flashcards be laminated so they can be used for years to come.

FLASHCARDS IN A BAG

Children love the mysterious act of putting their hand into a bag they can't see inside of and pulling something out. After pre-teaching a set of vocabulary flashcards, mix them up and put them in a bag.

Have students take turns putting their hand in the bag (make sure they can't peek in!) and pulling out a flashcard.

When students pull out the flashcard, ask a question like *What is it?* or *What do you have in your hand?* and have them answer (either one-word answers or complete sentences).

FLASHCARD MARCHING GAME

After pre-teaching a set of vocabulary flashcards, place them all around the edge of the table. (Actually, it is best to teach them as you place them around the table.)

Have the students stand around the table. Then say, *March! March!* and everyone marches around the table. Say, *Stop!*, and everyone has to slap their hand down on a card and say what it is. Then, leave all the cards in their original positions and repeat a few times.

Once students get used to this game, ask the students to take turns saying *March!* and *Stop!* You can take this one step further and ask students to choose a different action from marching, such as running, skipping, jumping, flying, dancing, etc.

MEMORY

For this game, you'll need a set of opposite adjectives cards, or two sets of identical flashcards. After pre-teaching the cards, place them face down on the table. A student turns over two cards and says what is on each card. If the cards are opposites (for example, *hot/cold*) or identical, the student gets to keep the cards. If not, she turns the cards face down again and leaves them in their original spot.

Students take turns doing this until all the cards have been matched up. The student with the most cards wins.

Note: This game can take a long time if you have many cards and/or younger students. To make the game easier and faster to play, divide up the cards while you pre-teach. Place a strip of paper or line up a few pens in the middle of the table and put each set on opposite sides.

FETCH THE CARD

For this game, you'll need a set of opposite adjectives cards or two sets of identical flashcards. Divide up the cards as you pre-teach them. Then place them face down on a table on the other side of the classroom or line them up against the wall.

Give each student one card from the other set and say, *Go!* Students have to find the matching card, bring both cards to you, and say what they are. Then, give them another card to match up, if any are left over.

Continue until all the cards have been matched up.

CROSS THE DANGEROUS BRIDGE!

Children get excited by stories that have a little danger, so use this to your advantage to motivate students to learn a full set of vocabulary words!

Pre-teach the flashcards as you line them up on the edge of a table. Then tell the students (in their native language, if they can't understand this much English) that the flashcards are a bridge that goes over dangerous water. If they can touch each flashcard and say what it is, then they can "cross the bridge to safety." If not, they "fall into the dangerous water" and have to pretend to swim to the end of the line.

Students that cross the bridge to safety have to cheer on the students that are trying for a second (or third!) time. While this game can be challenging, everyone ends up crossing the bridge and can feel a sense of accomplishment!

IV

GRAMMAR ACTIVITIES

When teaching grammar to children, keep in mind that they learn very differently from adults. Adults often learn grammar rules, analyze language that uses those rules, notice the rules when they read or listen, and try to internalize those rules. Sometimes teachers forget that children are not miniature adults and try to teach them grammar rules. This is not only developmentally inappropriate, it is also highly ineffective.

Children learn best when the language is presented in chunks instead of rules to memorize. Through exposure to those chunks, practicing them, and learning what they mean, they can learn English grammar naturally.

It takes a long time for children to internalize grammar.

One way to help is by exposing them to stories, songs, or chants that repeat a grammar pattern. Another way is to do activities where they can actively practice grammar forms in a meaningful way.

IS IT A ____? / IS IT AN ____? GUESSING GAME

Teach *a* and *an* with single noun vocabulary cards or a spread from a picture dictionary. Point out which nouns start with the letters *a, e, i, o,* or *u* and that you would use an rather than a in front of those cards.

Write the following on the board:

Is it a/an _____?

Yes, it is.
No, it isn't.

Be sure to point out to the children that *isn't* is what you get when you smash *is* and *not* together. (Words smashing into one another is more exciting than using technical terms like "contractions.")

Secretly choose one of the cards or one of the words in the picture dictionary. Lay out the cards or picture dictionary where all students can see it, and have them take turns asking you *Is it a ___?* or *Is it an ___?*

When a student guesses correctly and you answer *Yes, it is*, have her come to the front and secretly choose a card or a word from the picture dictionary to play the game again. Continue until all students have had a chance to come to the front.

SINGULAR/PLURAL NOUN PRACTICE

Take a stack of plural noun vocabulary flashcards. (At this beginning stage, just use nouns that are made plural by adding an "s" to the end.) Hold the flashcard up with one hand, and with the other hand, cover up all but one of the objects. Say the singular form of the noun. Then remove your hand and say the plural form of the noun.

For example, if you have a flashcard with many cats on it, cover up all but one cat with your hand and say *a cat*. Then remove your hand and say *cats*. Have the students repeat after you. Repeat with all flashcards.

Do the activity again, but this time, have only the students say the words. Then pass out a flashcard to each student and let them try covering up and removing the nouns as they say the singular and plural forms.

WHAT IS IT? / WHAT ARE THEY? AROUND THE TABLE ACTIVITY

This is great activity to do after students have learned the difference between singular and plural nouns, and the questions *What is it?* and *What are they?*

Mix up a set of singular noun flashcards and plural noun flashcards. Write the following on the board:

What is it? It's a / an _____.
What are they? They are _____.

Place the stack of mixed up cards on one end of the table and have students line up on the other side of the table. Hold up the first card. Ask *What is it?* or *What are they?*, and have students answer correctly in chorus.

Then have the first student in line come up to the stack, choose the next card, and ask the correct question. The rest of the class answers in chorus. Then that student goes to the end of the line and the next student comes up.

Repeat until all the cards have been asked about.

THIS/THAT, THESE/THOSE DRAWING ACTIVITY

This, that, these, and *those* are somehow difficult for young learners to remember, probably because they sound very similar, so it is important to take the time to practice these grammatical forms.

Draw a simple picture on the board; for example, a picture of a pencil. Stand next to the picture and say, *This is a pencil.* Then move far away from the board, point to the picture and say, *That is a pencil.* Go back to the board, draw another pencil, and say, *These are pencils.* Then move far away from the board, point to the picture, and say, *Those are pencils.*

Erase your picture and invite a student to come to the board, draw a new picture, and say the same kinds of sentences.

This activity will do more smoothly if you open a picture

dictionary to give students ideas of what to draw. To keep the student from spending too much time drawing (after all, this is an English activity, not an art project!), have the rest of the students count down from 20 to 1 as the student draws the picture.

HIS/HER DRAWING ACTIVITY

After teaching possessives, give each student a small piece of scrap paper and have them draw a simple picture of a noun of their choice. Students can choose a silly noun (for example, an elephant or an alien) if they wish.

Draw a simple picture of a boy on one side of the board and a girl on the other. Have the students stand in a line, holding their drawings. The first student will put her drawing to the board, using magnets or tape, near the boy or girl. If she puts her drawing near the boy, she will say, *This is his (noun)*. If she puts her drawing near the girl, she will say, *This is her (noun)*.

Once the students have put their drawings on the board, have them stand in line again, but this time point to another drawing (not their own) and make a sentence, and then remove the drawing from the board. Continue till all pictures are removed.

CAN YOU ____? ANIMAL GAME

Usually when we teach the question *Can you _____?*, we ask students what they can or can't do. Another way to practice this question is to ask students to pretend they are an animal and tell their classmates what kind of animal they are. Then the other students ask the student what kind of things they can and can't do, as that animal.

For example:

Student 1: I'm an elephant.
Student 2: Can you run?
Student 1: Yes, I can.
Student 3: Can you swim?
Student 1: Yes, I can.
Student 4: Can you jump?
Student 1: No, I can't.

V

COMBINATION ACTIVITIES

Too often, textbooks for children are organized so that each unit teaches a certain category of vocabulary, (e.g., colors or animals) and one or two grammar points. Each category of vocabulary is taught in isolation, and at no point are these put together to create new, meaningful opportunities for language production. While this might make for an easy to follow textbook, it goes against how language is really used.

Once students know some basic sets of vocabulary words and forms of grammar, what are you waiting for? Put them together into an activity where students can use what they know to interact with their classmates in English. Students will feel satisfied when they realize that they can already communicate in English, and this will motivate them to continue to study.

IT'S/THEY'RE, CLOTHING, AND OTHER THINGS WE WEAR

Review the difference between *It's* and *They're*. Review clothing vocabulary using flashcards. On one side of the board, write *It's*, and on the other side of the board write *They're*. Show each flashcard to the students and have them decide on which side of the board the flashcard should go; then prop that flashcard in the chalk tray.

For example, a flashcard of a hat should go under *It's*, but a flashcard of shoes should go under *They're*. Take extra time to show the students that *pants*, *shorts*, and *glasses* would go under the word *They're*, even though they seem like they would be singular nouns.

Once all the cards have been sorted, pick them up and show them one by one as you say the sentences together; for example, *It's a skirt* or *They're socks*.

Mix up all the cards and place them face down on the

table. Have students stand in a single-file line. The first student picks up a card, stands on the correct side of the board, says the sentence, sets the flashcard on the chalk tray, and goes to the end of the line.

Continue until there are no more cards.

HOUSE DICE GAME

Draw a simple outline of rooms in a house. Label the rooms as you pre-teach the vocabulary: *bedroom, bathroom, living room, kitchen,* and *dining room.*

Next to the house, write the following furniture or household objects and number them 1 – 12 as you pre-teach the vocabulary: *bed, dresser, lamp, bathtub, sink, sofa, television, rug, refrigerator, stove, table,* and *chairs.* Write the following sentence on the board: *The _____ is in the _____ .*

Give students a pair of dice. Students can roll one or two die and then say a sentence about the number of the household object that they rolled. For example, if they roll a 1, they say, *The bed is in the bedroom,* and then write a 1 in the bedroom on the board. If the number has already been written in the house, then their turn is over.

Some furniture or household objects can be in more than

one room; for example, a lamp could also be in the living room.

The game continues until all the numbers for the furniture or household objects have been written in correct rooms.

MY BIRTHDAY AND HOLIDAYS

Pre-teach months and ordinal numbers up to 31. Take an outdated wall calendar. Start with January and ask if any students have a birthday in that month. Students who do can write their name on the appropriate day. Then ask if any students know of holidays that are in that month (in January, one holiday would be New Year's Day on the 1st).

Continue with the rest of the months of the year.

Once all birthdays and holidays have been written down, go through the calendar month by month and say them in chorus. For example, *New Year's Day is January first. Maya's birthday is January seventh.*

PREPOSITIONS DICE GAME

Review the prepositions *in, on, under* (See Activity #20). Divide the board into three sections and write the numbers 1 – 6 in a horizontal line on the left side of each section.

Gather six different small classroom objects from the students, such as a pencil or eraser, and write the name of each object next to the numbers in the first section. In the middle section, write *in* next to numbers 1 and 2, *on* next to numbers 3 and 4, and *under* next to numbers 5 and 6. In the last section, write 6 different objects or pieces of furniture in the classroom, such as a closet or desk.

Demonstrate the activity. Roll a die three times. Then make a sentence out of the numbers you rolled, like this: *The (object from the first section) is (in, on, under) the (object or furniture in class).*

Then take the classroom object and place it where your sentence directed. Let each student roll, say a sentence, and put the objects in the correct place around the classroom.

ANIMAL BODY PARTS

Review animal and parts of the body vocabulary. Be sure to also review body parts only animals have, such as *wing* and *tail*.

Each student secretly decides what animal to be. Classmates ask them, *How many (body part) do you have?* questions to guess what animal they are.

Students can ask up to five questions, and then they have to guess!

ANIMAL GUESSING GAME

Review colors, sizes (*big, medium-sized, small*), body parts, and the adjectives *long* and *short*.

Write the following on the board:

1. It's _____. (big, medium-sized, small)
2. It's _____. (color)
3. It has a(n) _____ (big, small, long, short) _____ body part.

One student thinks of an animal and uses the three sentences on the board to give three clues about that animal. Other students try to guess what animal it is by asking *Is it a(n)* _____ *?*

The student who guesses correctly thinks of a new animal, and the game continues.

STORE

Students make different "stores," using different sets of flashcards. For example, one student could use vegetable flashcards to make a vegetable stand, or clothing cards to make a clothes shop. Other students are the customers, and pay for their items using play money.

If you don't have any play money, ask students to fold a piece of paper four times to make 16 small sections, cut them out, and make their own money.

Pre-teach and write the following questions and answers on the board that students can use when they "play store." You can practice them a few times through choral response before having students work independently.

> *A: May I help you?*
> *B: Yes, I'm looking for a _____.*
> *A: Here you are.*
> *B: How much is it?*
> *A: It's _____.*
> *B: I'll take it!*
> *A: Here you are.*
> *B: Thank you.*

Walk around the classroom to make sure the students are speaking English and to help them if necessary. However, don't interfere too much. Let them enjoy playing around in English. Once they start this activity, they won't want to stop!

TREASURE HUNT

Review the following phrases as you write them on the board: *Turn left, Turn right, Take (number) steps, Stop, It's (in, on, under) the* _____.

Make students close their eyes, and hide a small object somewhere in the classroom. Ask one student to stand up. Using the phrases written on the board, tell her where to go to find the object.

Once she has found the object, let her secretly hide the object again and ask another student to find it. Continue until all students have had a chance to hide and find the object.

VI

HOLIDAY ACTIVITIES

Holidays are fun times for children. A special date can be a great time to learn about traditions and festivals from other countries, such as Christmas or Halloween. It can also be a great time for children to learn more about their own holidays and how to talk about them in English.

Learning about holidays provides a great opportunity for students to learn about the world around them and the world outside their own country.

The holiday activities in this section are not only fun, they also take language learned in other parts of the book and put them into a new context. Students can review things such as phonics, body parts, shapes, and polite language while enjoying the excitement of the holiday.

CHRISTMAS PRESENTS

Take a plain envelope and draw a ribbon and bow on it to make it look like a gift box. Paste clip art of toys or other Christmas presents on a piece of paper and cut them up into small cards (or draw a picture of the toys or Christmas presents on small cards). Pre-teach the toys and Christmas presents.

Student 1 closes his eyes while Student 2 secretly chooses a card and puts it in the envelope. Student 1 opens her eyes. Student 2 hands the envelope to Student 1 and says, *Merry Christmas! This is for you!* Student 2 takes the envelope, pulls out the card and says, *Oh, it's a (toy or present)! Thank you!*

Continue until all students have had a chance to give and receive a present.

Christmas "stocking" with "gifts" inside

Variation: This can of course be adapted to suit other holidays where presents are given. Even a birthday can be used (*Happy birthday! This is for you!*).

CHRISTMAS PHONICS

Guessing the initial sounds of vocabulary words is a fun way to practice phonics and can also help students remember the word.

After teaching Christmas related vocabulary (for example, *Christmas tree, wreath, stocking, candy cane, Santa Claus, reindeer,* etc.), write a word on the board, but leave a blank for the first letter. Be sure to write the word low enough on the board for your young students to reach!

For example, if the word is *reindeer*, write __*eindeer*. Say the word a few times slowly, and then ask a student to guess the first letter. The student who guesses correctly can write the letter in the blank.

Continue with other vocabulary words and try to give all the students a chance to write the first letter.

JACK-O'-LANTERN BAG CRAFT/TRICK OR TREATING

Buy orange-colored paper bags for the students or buy plain paper bags and let them color or paint them orange. Review shapes and parts of the face. Tell the students what a jack-o'-lantern is, and then give them a piece of black construction paper. Tell them to make their own original jack-o'-lantern, using different shapes for the eyes, nose, and mouth.

When students have completed their bags, have them write their name on the back and tell you in English what they did. For example, *My jack-o'-lantern has square eyes, a triangle nose, and a heart mouth.* Collect the bags at the end of class.

On the class closest to Halloween (October 31), trick or treat with the class. Teach them how to say *Trick or treat!* When students hold out their bags and say *Trick or treat!*, put a small piece of candy in the bag.

If giving students candy is against school rules, print out clip art of candy, cut it up, and put that in their bags instead, or use a different reward such as stickers.

HALLOWEEN PHONICS

Guessing the initial sounds of vocabulary words is a fun way to practice phonics and can also help students remember the word.

After teaching Halloween related vocabulary (for example, *jack-o'-lantern*, *ghost*, *witch*, *vampire*, *candy*, *pumpkin*, *skeleton*, etc.), write a word on the board, but leave a blank for the first letter. Be sure to write the word low enough on the board for your young students to reach!

For example, if the word is *jack-o'-lantern*, write ___*ack-o'-lantern*. Say the word a few times slowly, and then ask a student to guess the first letter. The student who guesses correctly can write the letter in the blank.

Continue with other vocabulary words, and try to give all the students a chance to write the first letter.

MY HOLIDAY

Choose a holiday that is important in the country where you teach. Divide the board into four sections and label them: *I see.., I eat…, I wear…, I (do)…* .

Brainstorm with the students the things you see, eat, wear, and do for that holiday. If they only know how to say those things in their native language, teach them how to say them in English.

After brainstorming, give each student a small piece of paper and ask them to draw a picture of one thing about that holiday. Then have the students stand in a line with their drawings. Each student will put their picture in the correct section of the board, using a magnet or tape, and say a sentence about it.

For example, if they draw a picture of a special food they eat on the holiday, they will say, *I eat (special food)."*

Once all the students have put their drawings in the correct sections of the board, ask the students, *What do you see?*, *What do you eat?*, *What do you wear?*, *What do you do?*. Students will look at the drawings in each section and use them to answer the questions.

BONUS TIP!

51. **Describing Things in Nature**: Take the students outside to a park and ask them to gather plants and other things they find interesting, like leaves or rocks. Come back to the classroom and talk about what the students brought. If possible, bring in other things found in nature, such as cotton balls, natural sponges, or seashells.

Name each thing they gathered and write it on the board. If it is a countable noun, write *A* before the word (*A rock*); if it is a non-countable noun, use a capital letter for the first letter, since they will be using these words in a sentence.

Review the following adjectives and write them on the board: *smooth*, *rough*, *hard*, and *soft*. Pick up one of the objects and ask which word they would use to describe it. Then draw a simple picture of that object and write that sentence on the board. For example, *A rock is rough.*

Ask the students to draw pictures and write sentences about the objects. Once they have finished a sentence, ask them to raise their hand, read the sentence to you, and let you check it.

Many students need time to get used to writing a capital letter at the beginning of a sentence, leaving spaces between words, and putting a period at the end of the sentence, so be sure that they do these things correctly.

Printed in Great Britain
by Amazon